MW01234271

Personal Finance:

I'll Teach You

To Be

Rich

By Khaled Bouajaja

Content:

1. Introduction: Why Personal Finance Matters

Personal finance is essential because it provides a sense of security, stability, and freedom. When you have control over your finances, you can make informed decisions that align with your values and goals. Personal finance can help you achieve financial independence, reduce debt, build wealth, and enjoy a comfortable retirement.

Unfortunately, many people struggle with personal finance because of common misconceptions. Some believe that personal finance is too complicated or time-consuming to manage. Others assume that it's only for the wealthy or that they don't have enough money to make a difference. These myths can prevent people from taking control of their finances, leading to financial stress and anxiety.

In this book, we will explore the fundamentals of personal finance and provide practical strategies for managing your money. We will cover topics such as budgeting, saving, investing, debt management, and retirement planning. We will also address common misconceptions about personal finance and provide tips for overcoming them.

By the end of this book, you will have a solid understanding of personal finance and the confidence to take control of your finances. You will have the tools and knowledge to create a budget, reduce debt, save for the future, and achieve your financial goals.

Additionally, we will provide insights on how to make financial decisions that align with your values and priorities. We will also discuss the importance of setting financial goals and developing a plan to achieve them.

Furthermore, we will provide guidance on how to manage and reduce debt, including strategies for paying off credit card debt and student loans. We will also discuss the benefits of building an emergency fund, how to save for large purchases, and the importance of investing for long-term wealth creation.

Finally, we will cover retirement planning, including strategies for maximizing your retirement savings and understanding different types of retirement accounts. We will also discuss the importance of creating an estate plan to ensure that your assets are distributed according to your wishes.

In summary, this book aims to provide readers with a comprehensive understanding of personal finance and practical strategies for managing their money effectively. We hope that by reading this book, you will gain the knowledge and confidence to take control of your finances, achieve your financial goals, and enjoy a more secure and fulfilling life.

2. Setting Financial Goals

Setting financial goals is an essential first step in taking control of your finances. Financial goals can be short-term or long-term, and they can range from paying off debt to saving for a down payment on a house.

Short-term goals are typically those that you want to achieve within the next year or two. Examples of short-term financial goals include paying off credit card debt, building an emergency fund, and saving for a vacation.

Long-term goals are typically those that you want to achieve in five years or more. Examples of long-term financial goals include saving for retirement, buying a house, and paying for your child's education.

Once you have identified your financial goals, the next step is to create a budget that aligns with them. A budget is a plan for how you will allocate your income to cover your expenses, pay off debt, and save for your goals.

To create a budget that aligns with your goals, start by tracking your income and expenses for a few months. This will help you understand where your money is going and identify areas where you can cut back on spending.

Next, prioritize your expenses based on your goals. For example, if your goal is to pay off credit card debt, you may need to cut back on discretionary spending and redirect those funds towards debt repayment.

When it comes to paying off debt, there are several strategies you can use. One popular strategy is the debt snowball method, where you focus on paying off your smallest debt first while making minimum payments on your other debts. Once the smallest debt is paid off, you can use the extra money to pay off the next smallest debt and so on.

Another strategy is the debt avalanche method, where you focus on paying off the debt with the highest interest rate first while making minimum payments on your other debts. This method can save you money on interest payments in the long run.

In summary, setting financial goals, creating a budget, and using debt repayment strategies are essential steps in taking control of your finances. By prioritizing your expenses and aligning your budget with your goals, you can make progress towards achieving financial stability and freedom.

In addition to creating a budget and paying off debt, there are other strategies you can use to achieve your financial goals. These include:

1. Increasing your income: If you're struggling to make ends meet or save for your goals, consider finding ways to increase your income. This could involve negotiating a raise at work, taking on a side hustle, or starting a small business.
2. Automating your savings: To make saving easier, consider automating your savings contributions. Set up automatic transfers from your checking account to a savings account or investment account each month.
3. Investing for the long-term: Investing can be a powerful tool for building long-term wealth. Consider investing in low-cost index funds or ETFs to diversify your portfolio and minimize risk.
4. Revisiting and adjusting your goals: Your financial goals may change over time as your priorities and circumstances change. It's important to revisit your

goals periodically and adjust them as needed.

5. Seeking professional advice: If you're unsure about how to achieve your financial goals or need help managing your money, consider working with a financial advisor or planner. They can provide guidance and support to help you achieve your financial goals.

In summary, achieving your financial goals requires a combination of strategies, including increasing your income, automating your savings, investing for the long-term, and seeking professional advice. By taking these steps and staying committed to your goals, you can achieve financial stability and freedom.

It's also important to remember that achieving your financial goals is a journey, and it may take time and patience to see progress. Don't get discouraged if you encounter setbacks or obstacles along the way. Instead, focus on staying committed to your goals and taking small steps towards achieving them each day.

One helpful tool for staying motivated and accountable is to track your progress towards your goals. This can involve using a spreadsheet, a budgeting app, or a bullet journal to track your income, expenses, and savings each month. By seeing your progress over time, you can stay motivated and adjust your strategy as needed.

Another key factor in achieving your financial goals is to stay disciplined and avoid unnecessary spending. This doesn't mean that you have to live a completely frugal lifestyle, but rather that you should be mindful of your spending and prioritize your goals over short-term pleasures.

Ultimately, achieving your financial goals is about creating a balance between enjoying your life today and planning for your future. By setting clear goals, creating a budget, and using strategies to pay off debt and save for the future, you can achieve financial stability and freedom and enjoy a more fulfilling life.

In summary, the key takeaways from this section on setting financial goals are:

1. Identify your short-term and long-term financial goals.
2. Create a budget that aligns with your goals and prioritize your expenses accordingly.

3. Use strategies like the debt snowball or debt avalanche method to pay off debt.
4. Consider increasing your income, automating your savings, investing for the long-term, and seeking professional advice to achieve your goals.
5. Stay disciplined and avoid unnecessary spending to stay on track.

By following these steps and staying committed to your goals, you can achieve financial stability and freedom and live a more fulfilling life.

3. Saving and Investing

Saving and investing are critical components of achieving financial stability and building long-term wealth. In this section, we'll explore the importance of saving for emergencies, the different types of savings accounts and investment vehicles available, how to build a diversified investment portfolio, and strategies for maximizing returns while minimizing risk.

1. Saving for emergencies and unexpected expenses: One of the first steps to achieving financial stability is building an emergency fund. This should be a savings account that you can access easily in case of unexpected expenses or a loss of income. Experts recommend saving at least 3-6 months' worth of living expenses in an emergency fund.
2. Types of savings accounts and investment vehicles: There are several types of savings accounts and investment vehicles to consider, including:
- High-yield savings accounts: These accounts offer higher interest rates than

traditional savings accounts and can help your savings grow faster.

- Certificates of deposit (CDs): CDs are a low-risk investment that offer a fixed interest rate over a set period of time.
- Stocks and bonds: These are types of investments that can provide higher returns but also carry more risk.
- Mutual funds and exchange-traded funds (ETFs): These investment vehicles allow you to invest in a diversified portfolio of stocks and bonds without having to manage them individually.

3. Building a diversified investment portfolio: Diversification is key to minimizing risk in your investment portfolio. This involves spreading your investments across different asset classes and industries. A diversified portfolio can help you weather market fluctuations and achieve long-term growth.

4. Strategies for maximizing returns while minimizing risk: There are several strategies you can use to maximize returns while minimizing risk, including:

- Investing for the long-term: Historically, the stock market has provided higher returns over the long-term. By investing for the long-term, you can ride out short-term market fluctuations and achieve higher returns.

- Dollar-cost averaging: This involves investing a fixed amount of money at regular intervals, which can help you buy more shares when prices are low and fewer shares when prices are high.
- Rebalancing your portfolio: This involves periodically adjusting your investments to maintain your desired asset allocation and minimize risk.
- Investing in low-cost index funds and ETFs: These investment vehicles provide diversified exposure to the market at a low cost.

In summary, saving and investing are critical components of achieving financial stability and building long-term wealth. By building an emergency fund, choosing the right savings accounts and investment vehicles, building a diversified investment portfolio, and using strategies to maximize returns while minimizing risk, you can achieve your financial goals and enjoy a more fulfilling life.

It's important to remember that investing carries some level of risk, and it's important to choose investment vehicles that align with your risk tolerance and financial goals. It's also important to stay disciplined and avoid making emotional decisions based on short-term market fluctuations.

When it comes to saving for emergencies and unexpected expenses, it's a good idea to keep your emergency fund in a separate savings account that is easily accessible. This can help you avoid dipping into your long-term investments in case of unexpected expenses.

When building a diversified investment portfolio, it's important to consider your investment goals, risk tolerance, and time horizon. Working with a financial advisor or using online investment tools can help you build a portfolio that meets your needs and aligns with your goals.

Finally, when using strategies to maximize returns while minimizing risk, it's important to stay disciplined and avoid making emotional decisions based on short-term market fluctuations. By staying focused on your long-term goals and following a disciplined investment strategy, you can achieve financial stability and build long-term wealth.

One more important point to consider when it comes to saving and investing is the concept of compound interest. This is when your investments earn interest, and then the interest itself earns interest, leading to exponential growth over time.

By starting to save and invest early, even small amounts can grow significantly over time thanks to the power of compounding. This makes it important to start saving and investing as early as possible, even if it's just a small amount each month.

Additionally, it's important to periodically review your savings and investment strategy to ensure it aligns with your goals and risk tolerance. Your goals and circumstances may change over time, so it's important to adjust your savings and investment strategy accordingly.

Overall, saving and investing are important components of achieving financial stability and building long-term wealth. By following the strategies outlined in this section and staying disciplined and focused on your long-term goals, you can achieve financial freedom and live the life you desire.

4. Managing Credit and Debt

Managing credit and debt is an important aspect of personal finance that can have a significant impact on your financial well-being. In this section, we'll explore the importance of understanding credit scores and reports, strategies for improving your credit score, responsible use of credit cards, and techniques for paying off debt faster.

1. Understanding credit scores and reports: Your credit score is a numerical representation of your creditworthiness and is used by lenders to determine whether to approve you for credit and what interest rates to offer you. Your credit report contains information about your credit history, including your payment history, credit utilization, and length of credit history.

2. Strategies for improving your credit score: There are several strategies you can use to improve your credit score, including:

- Paying your bills on time: Payment history is the most important factor in determining your credit score, so it's important to make all of your payments on time.

- Reducing your credit utilization: Your credit utilization is the amount of credit you're using compared to the amount you have available. Aim to keep your credit utilization below 30% to improve your credit score.
- Checking your credit report for errors: Mistakes on your credit report can negatively impact your credit score, so it's important to review your report regularly and dispute any errors.
- Keeping old credit accounts open: The length of your credit history is also an important factor in determining your credit score, so keeping old credit accounts open can help improve your score.

3. Responsible use of credit cards: Credit cards can be a powerful tool for building credit and earning rewards, but it's important to use them responsibly. This means paying your bills on time and in full each month, avoiding carrying a balance, and not overspending.

4. Techniques for paying off debt faster: There are several techniques you can use to pay off debt faster, including:

- Snowball method: This involves paying off your smallest debt first and then using that momentum to pay off larger debts.
- Avalanche method: This involves paying off your debt with the highest interest rate first and then moving on to the next highest interest rate.
- Consolidation: This involves consolidating multiple debts into a single loan or credit card with a lower interest rate.

In summary, managing credit and debt is an important aspect of personal finance. By understanding credit scores and reports, using strategies to improve your credit score, using credit cards responsibly, and using techniques to pay off debt faster, you can achieve financial stability and build long-term wealth.

It's important to note that paying off debt can be a long and difficult process, but it's worth it in the end. By paying off your debts, you free up more money for savings and investments, which can help you achieve your long-term financial goals.

When it comes to credit cards, it's important to choose cards that align with your spending habits and financial goals. Look for cards with low interest rates, no annual fees, and rewards programs that offer cash back, points, or miles. However, it's important to use credit cards responsibly and not spend more than you can afford to pay off in full each month.

Finally, it's important to remember that improving your credit score and paying off debt takes time and discipline. By setting goals, creating a plan, and staying focused on your long-term financial goals, you can achieve financial stability and build long-term wealth.

Another important strategy for managing credit and debt is to prioritize which debts to pay off first. Generally, it's a good idea to pay off high-interest debt first, such as credit card debt or payday loans. These types of debt can have interest rates that are much higher than other types of debt, such as student loans or mortgages, and can quickly become unmanageable if left unpaid.

It's also important to create a realistic budget that includes debt repayment as a priority. This means allocating a portion of your income each month towards paying off debt, even if it means cutting back on other expenses. By prioritizing debt repayment in your budget, you can make consistent progress towards becoming debt-free.

In addition to these strategies, there are also resources available to help you manage your credit and debt. Credit counseling agencies, for example, can provide guidance and support for managing debt, creating a budget, and improving your credit score. They can also help negotiate with creditors to lower interest rates or establish payment plans.

In summary, managing credit and debt is an important aspect of personal finance that requires discipline, planning, and prioritization. By understanding your credit score and report, using responsible credit card habits, paying off high-interest debt first, creating a realistic budget, and seeking support when needed, you can achieve financial stability and build long-term wealth.

Sure, here are some easy-to-implement solutions for managing your personal finances:

1. Create a budget: Start by tracking your income and expenses for a month to see where your money is going. Then, create

a budget that allocates your income towards necessary expenses like housing, food, and bills, as well as savings and debt repayment. You can use budgeting apps like Mint or YNAB to help you get started.

2. Automate savings: Set up automatic transfers from your checking account to a savings account each month. This makes it easier to save and ensures that you're consistently setting money aside for your goals.

3. Pay off high-interest debt first: Identify any debts with high-interest rates, like credit card debt, and focus on paying them off first. This can save you money in the long run and help you become debt-free faster.

4. Use credit cards responsibly: Only charge what you can afford to pay off in full each month. This will help you avoid accumulating high-interest debt and damaging your credit score.

5. Invest in low-cost index funds: Consider investing in low-cost index funds, which offer diversification and are less expensive than actively managed funds. This can help you build long-term wealth and save money on fees.

6. Negotiate bills: Call your service providers and negotiate your bills to save money on things like cable, phone, and internet. Many providers offer discounts or promotions that you may not be aware of.

Remember, personal finance is a journey, and it's important to take small steps to achieve your goals. By implementing these easy-to-follow solutions, you can start taking control of your finances and build long-term wealth.

While there are many conventional strategies for credit and debt management, here are some more radical solutions that could be considered:

1. Debt consolidation: This involves taking out a loan to pay off all of your existing debts, leaving you with just one monthly payment. This can make it easier to manage your debt, but it's important to choose a loan with a lower interest rate than your existing debts.
2. Debt settlement: This involves negotiating with your creditors to settle your debts for less than what you owe. While this can reduce your debt, it can

also have a negative impact on your credit score.

3. Bankruptcy: This is a legal process where you declare that you are unable to pay your debts. While it can provide relief from overwhelming debt, it can also have serious long-term consequences, including a damaged credit score and difficulty obtaining credit in the future.

4. Selling assets: If you have valuable assets, like a car or a second home, you could consider selling them to pay off your debts. This can be a drastic measure, but it can provide immediate relief from debt.

It's important to note that these radical solutions should only be considered as a last resort, and should be thoroughly researched and discussed with a financial advisor or credit counselor before taking action. Additionally, it's important to address the underlying issues that led to the debt in the first place, such as overspending or living beyond your means. By making sustainable lifestyle changes and taking control of your finances, you can avoid the need for radical solutions in the future.

5. Real Estate and Homeownership

Real estate and homeownership can be a significant part of personal finance. Here are some important things to consider:

1. Buying vs Renting: One of the first decisions to make is whether to buy or rent a home. Owning a home can provide long-term financial benefits, such as building equity, tax deductions, and potential appreciation. However, it also comes with additional expenses and responsibilities, like mortgage payments, maintenance, and repairs. Renting provides flexibility and less financial responsibility, but can result in less long-term financial benefits.

2. Affordability: When considering purchasing a home, it's important to make sure it's affordable. As a general rule of thumb, your mortgage payment should not exceed 28% of your gross monthly income. Additionally, it's important to have enough money saved for a down payment, closing costs, and emergency funds.

3. Financing Options: There are various financing options available for purchasing a home, such as traditional mortgages, FHA loans, VA loans, and more. It's important to research and compare these options to find the best fit for your financial situation.
4. Home Equity: As you pay off your mortgage, you build equity in your home, which can be used for future expenses, such as home renovations or a down payment on a new home.
5. Real Estate Investing: Real estate can also be a way to invest and build wealth. This can include owning rental properties, flipping houses, or investing in real estate investment trusts (REITs).

It's important to carefully consider all aspects of real estate and homeownership before making any decisions. It's also important to work with a trusted real estate agent and mortgage lender to ensure you make informed decisions and get the best deal possible.

Buying and renting both have their own advantages and disadvantages. Here are some things to consider when deciding between buying and renting:

1. Affordability: Renting is generally more affordable in the short term, as it requires less upfront costs and often has lower monthly payments. Buying a home, on the other hand, can be more expensive in the short term, as it requires a down payment, closing costs, and ongoing maintenance expenses.

2. Long-term investment: Owning a home is generally seen as a long-term investment. Over time, the value of your home may appreciate, providing an opportunity for you to build equity and wealth. Renting, on the other hand, does not offer the same long-term investment opportunities.

3. Flexibility: Renting provides more flexibility than owning a home. If you need to move frequently or unexpectedly, it's much easier to break a lease than it is to sell a home. Additionally, renting may provide access to amenities and locations that are not available or affordable for homebuyers.

4. Maintenance and repairs: As a homeowner, you are responsible for all maintenance and repairs on your property, which can be costly and time-consuming. Renters, on the other hand,

generally have less responsibility for maintenance and repairs.

5. Control and customization: Homeowners have more control over their living space and the ability to customize it to their liking. Renters, on the other hand, may be limited in their ability to make changes to their living space.

Ultimately, the decision to buy or rent comes down to your individual financial situation, lifestyle, and long-term goals. It's important to carefully consider all factors and work with a trusted real estate agent or financial advisor before making any decisions.

Here are some steps to take when buying a home:

1. Determine your budget: Before you start looking for a home, determine how much you can afford to spend. Consider your income, expenses, and other financial obligations to determine your maximum budget.

2. Get pre-approved for a mortgage: Getting pre-approved for a mortgage can help you determine how much house you can afford and make you a

more attractive buyer to sellers. It also gives you a better idea of your interest rate and potential monthly mortgage payments.

3. Choose a real estate agent: Choose a reputable real estate agent who is familiar with the area where you want to buy. They can help you find homes that fit your budget and needs and guide you through the home buying process.

4. Start your home search: Use online listings, attend open houses, and work with your real estate agent to find homes that fit your needs and budget.

5. Make an offer: Once you find a home you want to buy, work with your real estate agent to make an offer. This may involve negotiating the price, contingencies, and other terms of the sale.

6. Have a home inspection: Before closing on the home, have a home inspection to identify any potential issues with the property. This can help you negotiate repairs or a lower price.

7. Close on the home: After your offer is accepted, work with your lender and real estate agent to finalize the sale. This may include getting a title search,

obtaining homeowners insurance, and signing closing documents.

Buying a home can be a complex process, but working with a trusted real estate agent and lender can help make it easier.

Buying a home is one of the biggest financial decisions you will make in your life. It's important to approach the process with careful planning and consideration to ensure that you make the best decisions for your financial future.

The first step in buying a home is to determine your budget. Consider your income, expenses, and other financial obligations to determine how much you can afford to spend on a home. Keep in mind that you will also need to factor in closing costs, property taxes, and ongoing maintenance expenses.

Once you have determined your budget, it's important to get pre-approved for a mortgage. This process involves working with a lender to determine how much you can borrow and at what interest rate. Getting pre-approved for a mortgage can help you determine how much house you can afford and make you a more attractive buyer to sellers.

Next, you will need to choose a real estate agent. A reputable real estate agent can help you find homes that fit your budget and needs and guide you through the home buying process. Look for an agent who is familiar with the area where you want to buy and has a good reputation in the industry.

Once you have a real estate agent, you can begin your home search. This may involve attending open houses, using online listings, and working with your agent to find homes that fit your budget and needs.

Once you find a home you want to buy, you will need to make an offer. This involves negotiating the price, contingencies, and other terms of the sale with the seller. Your real estate agent can help guide you through this process and ensure that you get the best deal possible.

Before closing on the home, it's important to have a home inspection. A home inspection can identify any potential issues with the property, such as structural problems or water damage. This can help you negotiate repairs or a lower price with the seller.

Finally, you will need to close on the home. This involves finalizing the sale with your lender and real estate agent. You will need to obtain a title search, obtain homeowners insurance, and sign closing documents. Once the sale is complete, you will officially own your new home.

Buying a home can be a complex process, but working with a trusted real estate agent and lender can help make it easier. Take your time and carefully consider your options to ensure that you make the best decisions for your financial future.

Managing a mortgage can be a significant financial responsibility, but there are several strategies you can use to make the process more manageable. Here are some tips for managing a mortgage:

1. Make your mortgage payments on time: Late payments can damage your credit score and result in costly fees and penalties. Set up automatic payments or create reminders to ensure that you never miss a payment.
2. Consider refinancing: If interest rates have fallen since you took out your mortgage, refinancing can help you save money on your monthly payments and reduce the overall cost of your loan.
3. Pay extra when possible: Making extra payments on your mortgage can help you pay off your loan faster and save money on interest over the life of the loan. Consider making an extra payment each year or increasing your monthly payments to pay off your loan faster.
4. Build an emergency fund: Unexpected expenses, such as home repairs or job loss, can make it difficult to make your mortgage payments. Building an emergency fund can help you cover

these expenses and avoid falling behind on your mortgage.

5. Consider a biweekly payment plan: Making biweekly payments can help you pay off your mortgage faster and reduce the amount of interest you pay over the life of the loan.

6. Monitor your credit score: Your credit score can impact your ability to qualify for a mortgage and the interest rate you pay. Check your credit report regularly and work to improve your score if necessary.

7. Consider a mortgage broker: A mortgage broker can help you find the best mortgage rates and terms for your financial situation. They can also help you navigate the application process and provide guidance on managing your mortgage.

By following these tips, you can manage your mortgage responsibly and ensure that you stay on track to achieving your financial goals.

A mortgage is a significant financial responsibility that can impact your financial well-being for decades to come. Managing a mortgage requires careful planning and a proactive approach to ensure that you stay on track with your payments and achieve your long-term financial goals.

One of the most important tips for managing a mortgage is to make your payments on time. Late payments can not only result in costly fees and penalties, but they can also damage your credit score, making it more difficult to obtain credit in the future. To ensure that you never miss a payment, consider setting up automatic payments or creating reminders for yourself.

Another strategy for managing a mortgage is to consider refinancing. If interest rates have fallen since you took out your mortgage, refinancing can help you save money on your monthly payments and reduce the overall cost of your loan. Refinancing can also help you pay off your mortgage faster by reducing your interest rate or changing the length of your loan.

Making extra payments on your mortgage is another effective strategy for managing your mortgage. By paying extra each month or making an extra payment each year, you can pay off your mortgage faster and save money on interest over the life of the loan. Consider using a mortgage calculator to determine how much you can save by making extra payments.

Building an emergency fund is another important strategy for managing a mortgage. Unexpected expenses, such as home repairs or job loss, can make it difficult to make your mortgage payments. By building an emergency fund, you can cover these expenses and avoid falling behind on your mortgage.

Consider a biweekly payment plan as well. Making biweekly payments can help you pay off your mortgage faster and reduce the amount of interest you pay over the life of the loan. Biweekly payments are structured so that you make half of your monthly payment every two weeks instead of the full amount once a month.

Monitoring your credit score is another important aspect of managing a mortgage. Your credit score can impact your ability to qualify for a mortgage and the interest rate you pay. Check your credit report regularly and work to improve your score if necessary.

Finally, consider working with a mortgage broker. A mortgage broker can help you find the best mortgage rates and terms for your financial situation. They can also help you navigate the application process and provide guidance on managing your mortgage.

In summary, managing a mortgage requires careful planning and a proactive approach. By following these tips, you can manage your mortgage responsibly and ensure that you stay on track to achieving your long-term financial goals.

Strategies for building equity and wealth through real estate

Real estate can be an effective way to build equity and wealth over time. Equity is the difference between the value of your property and the amount you owe on your mortgage. Building equity over time can help you build wealth, as you can use that equity to make a down payment on another property or sell the property and use the profits to invest in other assets.

Here are some strategies for building equity and wealth through real estate:

1. Make a larger down payment: Making a larger down payment when purchasing a property can help you build equity faster. By putting more money down, you'll have a smaller mortgage balance, which means you'll pay less interest over time and build equity more quickly.
2. Make extra payments: Making extra payments towards your mortgage each month can also help you build equity faster. By paying down the principal balance of your mortgage more quickly, you'll build equity faster and reduce the

amount of interest you pay over the life of the loan.

3. Renovate and improve your property: Renovating and improving your property can increase its value and help you build equity. By making strategic improvements that increase the value of your property, you can increase your equity and potentially sell the property for a profit in the future.

4. Rent out your property: Renting out your property can generate passive income and help you build equity over time. By renting out your property, you can use the rental income to pay down your mortgage and build equity more quickly.

5. Buy and hold properties: Buying and holding properties can be an effective way to build equity and wealth over time. By purchasing properties in up-and-coming neighborhoods, you can benefit from appreciation over time and build equity through property value increases.

6. Use a 1031 exchange: A 1031 exchange is a tax-deferred exchange that allows you to sell one property and use the proceeds to purchase another property without paying capital gains taxes. By

using a 1031 exchange, you can potentially build more equity and wealth over time by investing in higher-value properties.

7. Refinance your mortgage: Refinancing your mortgage can be a way to build equity and save money on interest payments. By refinancing at a lower interest rate or with a shorter loan term you pay over the life of the loan and build equity faster. For example, if you refinance from a 30-year mortgage to a 15-year mortgage, you'll pay off your mortgage more quickly and build equity faster. Just be sure to carefully evaluate the costs of refinancing, including closing costs and any prepayment penalties.

8. Invest in real estate investment trusts (REITs): Real estate investment trusts are a way to invest in real estate without actually owning property. REITs allow investors to pool their money together to invest in a portfolio of properties, generating income through rent and appreciation over time. Investing in REITs can be a way to diversify your real estate investments and potentially earn higher returns than traditional investments.

9. Participate in real estate crowdfunding: Real estate crowdfunding platforms allow investors to invest in real estate projects with a small amount of money, often as little as $1,000. Crowdfunding platforms allow investors to access deals that they may not be able to access on their own, and can provide higher returns than traditional investments.

10. Use a home equity line of credit (HELOC): A HELOC is a line of credit that allows you to borrow against the equity in your home. Using a HELOC can be a way to access the equity in your home to invest in other properties or to make other investments. However, it's important to carefully evaluate the risks of using a HELOC, as it can put your home at risk if you're unable to repay the loan.

Overall, building equity and wealth through real estate requires a strategic approach and a willingness to take calculated risks. By following these strategies, you can build equity over time and potentially achieve financial independence through real estate investing. However, it's important to carefully evaluate each investment opportunity and to work with a qualified real estate professional to minimize risks and maximize returns.

6. Starting and Growing a Business

Starting and growing a business is a complex process that requires careful planning, effective execution, and continuous innovation. Here's a more detailed look at the key steps and strategies involved in building a successful business.

1. Identify a market need: The first step in starting a business is to identify a market need or gap that your product or service can fill. This requires conducting market research to understand your target audience, their needs, and the competition. You can use online tools, surveys, and focus groups to gather insights and data that will help you make informed decisions about your business.

2. Develop a business plan: A business plan is a document that outlines your business goals, strategies, and financial projections. It's an important tool for securing financing and guiding your business decisions. A business plan typically includes an executive summary, a company description, market analysis, product or service descriptions, sales

and marketing strategies, financial projections, and a management plan.

3. Secure financing: Starting a business often requires financing, whether through loans, investments, or personal savings. Consider your options for financing and create a plan for how you'll use the funds to grow your business. You can explore traditional bank loans, government grants, angel investors, venture capitalists, or crowdfunding platforms.

4. Build a team: Building a strong team is essential for growing a successful business. Hire qualified individuals who share your vision and can help you achieve your goals. Develop a company culture that fosters creativity, innovation, and collaboration. You can also consider outsourcing certain tasks to freelancers or contractors to save costs and increase flexibility.

5. Create a strong brand: A strong brand can help your business stand out in a crowded market. Develop a unique brand identity that reflects your values and resonates with your target audience. Your brand should be consistent across all channels, including your website,

social media profiles, packaging, and advertising.

6. Market your business: Marketing is essential for attracting customers and growing your business. Develop a marketing plan that includes strategies for social media, advertising, and public relations. Consider your target audience, their preferences, and the most effective channels for reaching them. Monitor your results and adjust your strategies as needed.

7. Continuously innovate and improve: In order to stay competitive, it's important to continuously innovate and improve your products or services. Stay up-to-date on industry trends and invest in research and development to stay ahead of the curve. Listen to customer feedback and use it to refine your offerings.

8. Manage your finances: Effective financial management is essential for growing a successful business. Create a budget, monitor your cash flow, and invest in accounting software or professional services to help you stay on top of your finances. Keep track of your expenses and revenue, and regularly review your

financial statements to identify areas for improvement.

Starting and growing a business can be a challenging and rewarding journey. By following these steps and strategies, you can increase your chances of success and achieve financial independence through entrepreneurship.

Certainly! Starting and growing a business is a complex and rewarding process that requires careful planning, hard work, and a willingness to take risks. There are many factors to consider when starting and growing a business, from choosing a business structure and developing a business plan to hiring employees and securing financing.

One of the first steps in starting a business is choosing the right business structure. The most common options include sole proprietorship, partnership, limited liability company (LLC), and corporation. Each structure has its own unique benefits and drawbacks, and the choice will depend on factors such as the size of the business, the level of personal liability the owner is comfortable with, and tax considerations.

Developing a business plan is another crucial step in starting a business. A well-written business plan can help entrepreneurs articulate their vision, identify target customers, and establish clear goals and milestones. It can also help secure funding from investors and lenders. A business plan typically includes an executive summary, a company description, a market analysis, a product or service line description, a marketing and sales strategy, and a financial plan.

Once a business is up and running, there are many challenges and opportunities to navigate. One of the biggest challenges is managing growth while maintaining quality and customer satisfaction. Entrepreneurs must be able to balance their ambitions with the realities of their resources, and prioritize strategic investments that will support long-term growth.

Other key factors in growing a business include building a strong team, developing effective marketing strategies, and managing finances. Hiring talented employees and providing ongoing training and support can help ensure the success of a growing business. Developing a strong brand identity, identifying target audiences, and leveraging social media and other marketing channels can also help businesses expand their reach and build customer loyalty. Managing finances effectively, including cash flow, debt, and taxes, is also critical for long-term success.

Overall, starting and growing a business is a complex and challenging process, but one that can be highly rewarding for those with the vision, drive, and determination to succeed. Successful entrepreneurs are able to balance their creativity and passion with a strong understanding of the market, a willingness to adapt to changing conditions, and a commitment to ongoing learning and growth.

In addition to the factors mentioned above, there are several other important considerations when starting and growing a business. One is the need to stay current with technology and industry trends. This means staying up to date with the latest tools, software, and hardware that can help streamline business processes and improve efficiency. It also means staying informed about industry trends, consumer behavior, and emerging markets that can provide new opportunities for growth.

Another important factor in starting and growing a business is the ability to build and maintain strong relationships with customers, suppliers, and other stakeholders. This requires excellent communication skills, a customer-focused approach, and a commitment to delivering high-quality products and services.

Finally, it's important for entrepreneurs to be flexible and adaptable in the face of changing market conditions and unforeseen challenges. This means being willing to pivot and adjust business strategies as needed, and being open to feedback and constructive criticism from customers, employees, and other stakeholders.

Overall, starting and growing a business requires a combination of strategic planning, hard work, creativity, and adaptability. By focusing on key areas such as business structure, business planning, team building, marketing, and financial management, entrepreneurs can increase their chances of success and build a thriving and sustainable business.

Assessing your business idea and market viability is a critical first step when starting and growing a business. It involves researching and analyzing various factors to determine whether your business idea is viable and has the potential to succeed in the market.

One key factor to consider is the demand for your product or service. Is there a need or desire for what you're offering? What are the demographics of your target audience, and how much are they willing to pay for your product or service? Conducting market research and gathering customer feedback can help you answer these questions and validate your business idea.

You also need to consider the competition in your industry. Who are your competitors, and what are their strengths and weaknesses? What sets your business apart from theirs, and how can you differentiate yourself in the market? By understanding the competitive landscape, you can identify opportunities to carve out a niche and position your business for success.

Another key factor to consider is the cost of starting and running your business. What are your startup costs, and how much will it cost to maintain and grow your business over time? Do you have the necessary financial resources to support your business until it becomes profitable? Understanding your financials and developing a comprehensive business plan can help you anticipate and manage these costs.

Ultimately, assessing your business idea and market viability requires a comprehensive approach that takes into account a range of factors, from market demand and competition to financial feasibility and strategic positioning. By conducting thorough research and analysis, you can increase your chances of success and build a business that is both sustainable and profitable.

Developing a comprehensive business plan

Once you've assessed your business idea and market viability, the next step in starting and growing a business is to develop a comprehensive business plan. A business plan serves as a roadmap for your business and outlines your goals, strategies, and tactics for achieving them.

Your business plan should include a detailed analysis of your target market, competition, and industry trends, as well as a description of your products or services and their unique selling points. It should also outline your marketing and sales strategies, as well as your financial projections and funding requirements.

In addition to helping you secure funding and investors, a business plan can also serve as a tool for measuring your progress and making strategic adjustments along the way. By setting clear goals and milestones, and regularly reviewing and revising your plan as needed, you can ensure that your business stays on track and adapts to changes in the market.

Securing funding and managing finances

Securing funding is often a critical component of starting and growing a business, as it allows you to invest in the resources and infrastructure necessary to get your business off the ground. There are a variety of funding options available, from traditional bank loans and angel investors to crowdfunding platforms and government grants.

Once you've secured funding, managing your finances is critical for ensuring the long-term success of your business. This includes developing and tracking budgets, managing cash flow, and forecasting revenue and expenses. It's also important to establish sound accounting practices and hire professionals, such as bookkeepers and accountants, to help you manage your finances.

Building a team and managing human resources

As your business grows, building a strong team and managing human resources becomes increasingly important. This includes hiring the right people, developing and implementing HR policies and procedures, and providing ongoing training and professional development opportunities.

It's also important to foster a positive and inclusive work culture that values diversity, equity, and inclusion. By creating a supportive and collaborative work environment, you can attract and retain top talent and build a strong foundation for your business's success.

Managing operations and scaling your business

Managing your business's day-to-day operations is critical for ensuring its continued success. This includes developing and implementing operational processes and procedures, managing supply chain and logistics, and monitoring key performance indicators (KPIs) to track your progress and identify areas for improvement.

As your business grows, scaling becomes a key priority. This involves expanding your operations and infrastructure to accommodate increased demand, while also maintaining quality and efficiency. It may involve expanding into new markets or product lines, developing new partnerships and collaborations, or implementing new technology and systems.

Overall, starting and growing a business requires careful planning, resourcefulness, and perseverance. By assessing your business idea and market viability, developing a comprehensive business plan, securing funding and managing finances, building a strong team and managing human resources, and managing operations and scaling your business, you can build a successful and sustainable business that meets the needs of your customers and stakeholders.

Financing options for new businesses

Financing is one of the biggest challenges for new businesses. There are many ways to finance a startup, but not all options are right for every entrepreneur. Here are some financing options to consider:

1. Personal Savings: If you have enough money saved up, you can use your own funds to start your business. This is the least risky option because you won't have to pay interest or give up any ownership stake in your company.

2. Friends and Family: You can also ask friends and family to invest in your business. This can be a good option if you don't have enough personal savings or don't qualify for a loan from a bank.

3. Business Loans: There are many types of business loans available from banks and other lenders. You'll need to have a solid business plan and good credit to qualify for a loan. Interest rates can vary widely depending on the lender and your credit score.

4. Crowdfunding: Crowdfunding has become a popular way for startups to raise funds. Platforms like Kickstarter and Indiegogo allow entrepreneurs to pitch their ideas to a large audience and ask for donations or pre-orders.

5. Angel Investors: Angel investors are wealthy individuals who invest in startups in exchange for equity. They usually invest smaller amounts than venture capitalists and are more likely to invest in early-stage startups.

6. Venture Capitalists: Venture capitalists are investors who provide large amounts of capital to startups in exchange for equity. They typically invest in companies that have already shown some traction and have the potential for significant growth.

It's important to remember that each financing option has its own advantages and disadvantages. You should carefully consider your options and choose the one that best fits your business and financial goals.

Starting and growing a business requires financial resources, which can come from various sources. Financing options for new businesses can be broadly categorized into two categories: debt and equity financing.

Debt financing involves borrowing money that needs to be repaid with interest. This can be in the form of a loan or a line of credit. Debt financing is a popular option for startups because it allows them to retain ownership of the company and its profits. However, it also requires the business to make regular payments, which can be a challenge in the early stages when revenue is limited.

Equity financing, on the other hand, involves selling a portion of the business in exchange for funds. This can be in the form of angel investors, venture capitalists, or crowdfunding. Equity financing can be a good option for businesses that have high growth potential but don't have the cash flow to support debt financing. However, it also means that the business owner will have to share ownership and profits with investors.

Personal savings and friends and family are also popular financing options for new businesses. Personal savings are often the least risky option because it doesn't involve any interest payments or giving up ownership. However, it can be challenging to come up with enough funds to start a business.

Friends and family can also be a good source of funding for startups. However, it's important to make sure that the terms of the investment are clearly defined and agreed upon to avoid potential conflicts down the line.

Overall, choosing the right financing option for your business will depend on various factors, including your business model, financial goals, and risk tolerance. It's important to carefully evaluate each option and choose the one that best aligns with your long-term vision for your business.

Managing cash flow and finances for small businesses

Managing cash flow and finances is crucial for the success of any small business. Here are some tips on how to effectively manage cash flow and finances for your business:

1. Create a cash flow projection: A cash flow projection will help you understand when cash is coming in and going out of your business. This will allow you to make informed decisions about spending and investments.

2. Monitor and manage expenses: Keep track of all expenses and identify areas where you can reduce costs. It's important to prioritize expenses and avoid overspending, especially in the early stages of your business.

3. Separate personal and business finances: Keep your personal and business finances separate. This will make it easier to track expenses and file taxes. It will also help you maintain a professional image and build credibility with lenders and investors.

4. Build an emergency fund: Set aside funds to cover unexpected expenses or a temporary drop in revenue. This will give you a buffer and help you avoid cash flow problems.

5. Stay on top of invoicing and accounts receivable: Make sure you invoice promptly and follow up on late payments. Consider offering incentives for early payments or penalties for late payments.

6. Maintain good relationships with suppliers and vendors: Pay your bills on time and negotiate favorable payment terms. This will help you build good relationships with suppliers and vendors and potentially lead to discounts or better terms in the future.

7. Seek professional advice: Consider working with an accountant or financial advisor who can provide guidance and help you make informed financial decisions.

By effectively managing cash flow and finances, you can ensure the long-term success of your small business.

Sure! Managing cash flow and finances is crucial for the success of any small business, as it helps businesses plan for the future and make informed decisions. By effectively managing cash flow and finances, businesses can avoid cash flow problems and ensure long-term success.

One important step in managing cash flow is to create a cash flow projection. A cash flow projection will help you understand when cash is coming in and going out of your business, which will allow you to make informed decisions about spending and investments. It can also help you identify potential cash flow problems before they occur, so you can take corrective action in advance.

Another important aspect of managing finances for a small business is to monitor and manage expenses. By keeping track of all expenses and identifying areas where you can reduce costs, you can prioritize expenses and avoid overspending, especially in the early stages of your business. This can help you conserve cash and ensure the longevity of your business.

It is also important to separate personal and business finances. By keeping your personal and business finances separate, you can more easily track expenses and file taxes. It will also help you maintain a professional image and build credibility with lenders and investors.

Another key strategy is to build an emergency fund. Setting aside funds to cover unexpected expenses or a temporary drop in revenue can give you a buffer and help you avoid cash flow problems. This can help you weather unexpected financial challenges and maintain the financial health of your business.

Finally, staying on top of invoicing and accounts receivable is essential. By invoicing promptly and following up on late payments, you can ensure a steady stream of revenue. It is also important to consider offering incentives for early payments or penalties for late payments.

Overall, effectively managing cash flow and finances is critical for the long-term success of any small business. Seeking professional advice from an accountant or financial advisor can also be helpful in making informed financial decisions.

Strategies for scaling and growing your business over time

Scaling and growing a business over time requires careful planning and strategic execution. Here are some strategies that can help you scale and grow your business:

1. Set clear goals and objectives: You should have a clear understanding of what you want to achieve with your business and set specific, measurable, achievable, relevant, and time-bound (SMART) goals. This will help you stay focused and track your progress over time.

2. Develop a growth strategy: Identify the most effective strategies for growing your business, such as expanding your customer base, entering new markets, or introducing new products or services. Develop a detailed plan for executing your growth strategy, including timelines, budgets, and resources.

3. Invest in technology and automation: Technology and automation can help you

streamline your operations, reduce costs, and increase efficiency. Identify the areas of your business that can benefit from automation, such as customer service, marketing, or production, and invest in the right tools and software.

4. Build a strong team: Your employees are one of the most valuable assets of your business. Hire talented and motivated employees, invest in their training and development, and create a positive and supportive work environment. This will help you attract and retain top talent and build a strong and productive team.

5. Focus on customer satisfaction: Your customers are the lifeblood of your business, and their satisfaction is crucial for your success. Focus on delivering high-quality products and services, providing excellent customer service, and building long-term relationships with your customers.

6. Expand your network: Networking can help you connect with potential customers, partners, and investors, and open up new opportunities for your business. Attend industry events, join professional associations, and participate in online communities to expand your network and build relationships.

7. Monitor your financials: As your business grows, it becomes even more important to monitor your financials closely. Keep track of your cash flow, monitor your expenses, and regularly review your financial statements. This will help you make informed decisions about investments, expansion, and other strategic initiatives.

By implementing these strategies, you can scale and grow your business over time and achieve long-term success. Remember that growth requires persistence, patience, and a willingness to take calculated risks.

Once you have successfully launched your business and established a strong customer base, you may start to consider scaling and growing your business to increase profitability and market share. Here are some strategies for scaling and growing your business over time:

1. Expand your product or service offerings: Consider diversifying your product or service offerings to appeal to a wider audience. This may involve conducting market research to identify new customer needs and preferences or developing

new products or services that complement your existing offerings.

2. Increase your marketing efforts: Invest in targeted marketing campaigns to raise awareness of your brand and attract new customers. This may involve utilizing social media platforms, paid advertising, email marketing, or other digital marketing channels to reach your target audience.

3. Hire additional staff: As your business grows, you may need to hire additional staff to help manage increased demand. Be sure to recruit individuals who share your company's values and vision and have the skills and experience necessary to contribute to your growth.

4. Streamline operations: As your business expands, it's important to regularly assess your operations and identify areas for improvement. This may involve automating certain processes, implementing new technologies, or outsourcing certain tasks to free up time and resources for more strategic initiatives.

5. Establish strategic partnerships: Consider establishing strategic partnerships with other businesses or organizations that can help you reach new customers or expand your reach in new markets. This may involve partnering with complementary businesses or organizations that share your target audience or values.

6. Explore new markets: Consider expanding into new markets to diversify your revenue streams and reduce dependence on a single market or customer segment. This may involve conducting market research to identify new opportunities or developing new products or services tailored to the needs of new customer segments.

Ultimately, scaling and growing your business requires a strategic approach and a willingness to take risks and adapt to changing market conditions. By carefully assessing your options and investing in the right areas, you can position your business for long-term success and profitability.

7. Planning for Retirement

Planning for retirement is an important aspect of personal finance that can help ensure financial stability and security in one's later years. Retirement planning involves setting financial goals and developing a plan to achieve those goals.

One of the first steps in retirement planning is to estimate how much money you will need in retirement. This will depend on a number of factors, including your current age, your retirement age, your life expectancy, and your expected retirement lifestyle.

Once you have an estimate of how much money you will need in retirement, you can start developing a plan to save and invest for that goal. This may involve setting up retirement accounts such as 401(k)s or IRAs, contributing regularly to those accounts, and investing in a diversified portfolio that balances risk and reward.

It's also important to consider other factors that may affect your retirement plans, such as Social

Security benefits, healthcare costs, and inflation. In some cases, it may be necessary to adjust your retirement plans to account for these factors.

Retirement planning is not a one-time event, but rather a process that should be revisited periodically to ensure that your plans are on track and to make any necessary adjustments. This may involve reviewing your investment portfolio, adjusting your savings rate, or reevaluating your retirement lifestyle goals.

Overall, retirement planning is an important aspect of personal finance that can help ensure financial security and stability in one's later years. With careful planning and regular monitoring, it is possible to achieve a comfortable and fulfilling retirement.

In addition to saving and investing for retirement, it's also important to consider ways to manage your retirement income once you do retire. This may involve creating a retirement budget, managing your investment portfolio to balance risk and reward, and exploring options for generating additional retirement income such as part-time work or rental income.

Another important aspect of retirement planning is estate planning. This involves creating a plan for how your assets will be distributed after your death, as well as considering issues such as healthcare directives and powers of attorney. Proper estate planning can help ensure that your wishes are carried out and that your loved ones are taken care of after you pass away.

Retirement planning can be complex and may involve a number of different financial and legal considerations. It's important to seek the guidance of a financial professional or attorney to ensure that you are making informed decisions and taking advantage of all available resources and strategies.

Overall, planning for retirement is an important aspect of personal finance that should not be overlooked. With careful planning, regular monitoring, and professional guidance, it is possible to achieve a comfortable and fulfilling retirement that meets your financial and lifestyle goals.

Planning for retirement involves making sure that you have enough money to support your lifestyle and expenses during your retirement years. This typically involves saving and investing over a long period of time in order to build up a nest egg that can be used to generate income during retirement.

There are a number of different factors that should be taken into account when planning for retirement, including your current age, your expected retirement age, your desired retirement lifestyle, and any sources of retirement income that you may have (such as pensions or Social Security).

One of the key steps in planning for retirement is creating a retirement budget. This involves estimating your expenses during retirement and comparing them to your expected income sources in order to determine how much you will need to save and invest in order to achieve your retirement goals.

Another important aspect of retirement planning is managing your investment portfolio. This involves choosing investments that are appropriate for your risk tolerance and investment goals, monitoring your portfolio regularly to ensure that it remains aligned with your objectives, and making adjustments as needed to account for changes in your financial situation or market conditions.

Finally, estate planning is an important aspect of retirement planning. This involves creating a plan for how your assets will be distributed after your death, as well as considering issues such as healthcare directives and powers of attorney.

Overall, planning for retirement is an important part of personal finance that requires careful consideration of a number of different factors. By taking the time to plan and prepare, it is possible to achieve a comfortable and fulfilling retirement that meets your financial and lifestyle goals.

Understanding different retirement plans (401(k), IRA, etc.)

When planning for retirement, it's important to understand the different retirement plans that are available to you. Here are some of the most common types of retirement plans:

1. 401(k): A 401(k) is a type of retirement plan that is offered by many employers. Employees can contribute a portion of their salary to the plan, and these contributions are tax-deferred, meaning that they are not taxed until the money is withdrawn during retirement. Employers may also offer matching contributions to the plan, which can help to boost retirement savings.

2. Traditional IRA: An Individual Retirement Account (IRA) is a type of retirement plan that allows individuals to save for retirement on a tax-deferred basis. Contributions to a traditional IRA are tax-deductible, and the money is not taxed until it is withdrawn during retirement.

3. Roth IRA: A Roth IRA is similar to a traditional IRA, but contributions are made with after-tax dollars. The money grows tax-free, and withdrawals during retirement are also tax-free. Roth IRAs are a good option for individuals who expect to be in a higher tax bracket during retirement.

4. Simplified Employee Pension (SEP) IRA: A SEP IRA is a retirement plan that is designed for small businesses and self-employed individuals. Contributions to the plan are tax-deductible, and the money is not taxed until it is withdrawn during retirement.

5. Defined Benefit Plan: A defined benefit plan is a type of retirement plan that is typically offered by employers. With a defined benefit plan, the employer guarantees a specific retirement benefit to the employee, based on factors such as salary and length of employment.

6. Social Security: Social Security is a government-administered retirement benefit program that provides retirement, disability, and survivor benefits to eligible individuals. The amount of the benefit is based on factors such as the individual's earnings history and the age at which they begin receiving benefits.

Understanding the different types of retirement plans can help you to make informed decisions about how to save for retirement and which types of plans may be most appropriate for your financial situation and goals. It's important to work with a financial advisor to develop a comprehensive retirement plan that takes into account all of your income sources, expenses, and investment strategies.

Retirement plans are savings and investment vehicles that are specifically designed to help individuals save for retirement. These plans come in many different forms, but the most common ones are 401(k)s and Individual Retirement Accounts (IRAs).

A 401(k) plan is a type of employer-sponsored retirement plan that allows employees to contribute a portion of their salary to the plan, often with matching contributions from their employer. The contributions are made on a pre-tax basis, which means that they are deducted from the employee's taxable income, thereby reducing their tax liability. The contributions are then invested in a variety of investment options, such as mutual funds or stocks, which can grow tax-free until the money is withdrawn in retirement.

An IRA is an individual retirement account that individuals can open and contribute to on their own, without any employer involvement. There are two types of IRAs: Traditional and Roth. With a Traditional IRA, contributions are made on a pre-tax basis, and the funds grow tax-deferred until retirement. Withdrawals in retirement are taxed as ordinary income. With a Roth IRA, contributions are made on an after-tax basis, but the funds grow tax-free and qualified withdrawals in retirement are tax-free as well.

Other types of retirement plans include Simplified Employee Pension (SEP) plans, Simple IRA plans, and Keogh plans, which are geared towards self-employed individuals.

Understanding these retirement plans is important for individuals to make informed decisions about which plan(s) to use to save for their retirement, and how much to contribute.

Strategies for maximizing retirement savings

Planning for retirement is a critical financial goal that everyone should prioritize, regardless of age. Retirement planning involves setting aside money to support yourself financially in your golden years, when you are no longer working. It is essential to plan and save for retirement as early as possible to maximize your savings.

One way to save for retirement is through retirement plans, such as a 401(k) or an individual retirement account (IRA). These plans offer tax benefits and provide a way to save for retirement while working. Employers often offer 401(k) plans, which allow employees to contribute a percentage of their salary to the account, and the employer may also contribute a matching amount. IRAs, on the other hand, are individual retirement accounts that can be opened by anyone and can offer tax benefits. There are different types of IRAs, such as traditional IRAs and Roth IRAs, each with unique tax benefits.

To maximize your retirement savings, you should contribute as much as possible to these retirement accounts, up to the annual contribution limits. Additionally, it is essential to invest your retirement savings in a diversified portfolio of stocks, bonds, and other assets, depending on your risk tolerance and retirement goals. Diversifying your investments helps to minimize risk and maximize potential returns.

Another strategy for maximizing retirement savings is to delay retirement as long as possible. By continuing to work and earn income, you can continue to contribute to your retirement accounts, and your savings will continue to grow. Additionally, delaying retirement can increase your Social Security benefits, which can provide a valuable source of income in retirement.

Finally, it is important to regularly review and adjust your retirement plan as your financial situation and retirement goals change. By keeping a close eye on your retirement savings and adjusting your plan as needed, you can ensure that you are on track to achieve a comfortable and secure retirement.

There are several strategies that individuals can use to maximize their retirement savings:

1. Start saving early: The earlier you start saving for retirement, the more time your money has to grow. Starting early also allows you to take advantage of compound interest, which can significantly increase the value of your savings over time.

2. Contribute regularly: Making regular contributions to your retirement account, such as a 401(k) or IRA, can help you accumulate a significant amount of savings over time. Many retirement plans also offer employer matching contributions, which can further increase your retirement savings.

3. Increase your contributions over time: As your income grows, consider increasing your contributions to your retirement account. This will help you take advantage of your higher income and ensure that you are saving enough to meet your retirement goals.

4. Diversify your investments: Diversifying your investments across different asset classes, such as stocks, bonds, and real estate, can help reduce your overall risk and increase your potential for higher returns.

5. Minimize fees: Pay attention to the fees associated with your retirement accounts and investment vehicles. High fees can significantly reduce your returns over time, so it's important to choose investments with low fees whenever possible.

6. Delay retirement if possible: If you can delay your retirement, even for a few years, you can significantly increase your retirement savings. This is because you'll have more time to contribute to your retirement accounts and allow your investments to grow.

7. Consider working with a financial advisor: A financial advisor can help you create a retirement plan that takes into account your individual goals and circumstances. They can also help you choose investments and create a personalized retirement savings strategy.

Preparing for retirement income and expenses

Preparing for retirement income and expenses is an important part of retirement planning. To ensure that you are financially prepared for your retirement, you need to understand your retirement income sources, estimate your retirement expenses, and create a retirement budget.

Retirement Income Sources:

Retirement income can come from various sources, such as social security benefits, pension plans, personal savings, and investments. It is important to estimate how much income you can expect to receive from each source and determine if it will be sufficient to cover your retirement expenses.

Retirement Expenses:

Retirement expenses can be broken down into two categories: essential and discretionary expenses. Essential expenses include items such as housing, healthcare, and basic living expenses, while discretionary expenses include items such as travel and entertainment. You should estimate your expected expenses for each category and ensure that your retirement income sources are sufficient to cover these expenses.

Retirement Budget:

Creating a retirement budget can help you plan your expenses and manage your retirement income sources effectively. Your retirement budget should include all of your expected retirement expenses, as well as any other sources of income you may have, such as rental income or part-time work. This will help you determine how much you need to save to achieve your retirement goals.

In addition to the above strategies, it is also important to consider factors such as inflation, taxes, and healthcare costs when planning for retirement income and expenses. By taking a comprehensive approach to retirement planning, you can ensure that you are financially prepared for your retirement years.

Planning for Retirement:

Preparing for retirement income and expenses

As you approach retirement, it's important to start thinking about how you'll generate income and manage your expenses. Here are some key strategies to consider:

1. Determine your retirement income sources: Before you retire, you'll want to take stock of all of your potential sources of income, including Social Security, pension plans, retirement accounts, and any other investments. This will help you understand how much income you can expect to have in retirement and will inform your budgeting decisions.

2. Create a retirement budget: Once you understand your expected income, you'll want to create a budget that outlines your expected expenses in retirement. This should include your basic living expenses, such as housing, food, and healthcare, as well as any discretionary spending you plan to do in retirement.

3. Consider healthcare costs: Healthcare costs are likely to be a significant expense in retirement, so it's important to factor these into your budget. Consider purchasing a Medicare supplemental insurance policy to help cover some of these costs.

4. Review your investment portfolio: As you near retirement, it's important to review your investment portfolio to ensure that it is appropriately balanced for your retirement goals. You may want to shift your investments to a more conservative allocation to protect your savings.

5. Consider delaying Social Security: Delaying your Social Security benefits until you reach your full retirement age or even beyond can help maximize your monthly benefit payments. If you're able to continue working, you may also be able to delay taking Social Security and continue contributing to your retirement accounts.

By taking these steps, you can help ensure that you're prepared for retirement and have the financial resources you need to enjoy your retirement years.

Managing retirement assets and withdrawals

Managing retirement assets and withdrawals is a critical aspect of retirement planning. There are several strategies that retirees can use to ensure that their retirement assets last throughout their retirement years.

One common strategy is to use the 4% rule. This rule states that retirees can withdraw 4% of their retirement assets in the first year of retirement and adjust this amount for inflation each year thereafter. For example, if a retiree has $1 million in retirement assets, they can withdraw $40,000 in the first year of retirement.

Another strategy is to use a retirement income floor. This involves creating a guaranteed stream of income that covers essential expenses such as housing, food, and healthcare. This can be accomplished through a combination of Social Security, pensions, and annuities.

Retirees may also want to consider a bucket strategy, which involves dividing retirement assets into different "buckets" based on the time horizon for each bucket. For example, a retiree may have a short-term bucket for expenses in the next 1-2 years, a mid-term bucket for expenses in the next 3-7 years, and a long-term bucket for expenses beyond 7 years.

Finally, retirees should carefully consider the tax implications of their withdrawals. Withdrawals from traditional 401(k)s and IRAs are taxed as ordinary income, while withdrawals from Roth accounts are tax-free. Retirees may want to consult with a financial advisor or tax professional to determine the most tax-efficient withdrawal strategy for their individual circumstances.

Sure, here are some additional details on managing retirement assets and withdrawals:

Once you have reached retirement age and start receiving retirement income, it is important to manage your retirement assets wisely to ensure that your money lasts throughout your retirement. Here are some tips for managing your retirement assets and withdrawals:

1. Review and adjust your investment portfolio: As you enter retirement, you may want to adjust your investment portfolio to reduce risk and ensure that you have enough income to cover your expenses. Consider working with a financial advisor to create a retirement income plan that balances risk and income.

2. Withdrawal strategies: You will need to decide how much to withdraw from your retirement accounts each year. There are different strategies for determining withdrawal amounts, including the 4% rule, which suggests withdrawing 4% of your retirement assets each year, and the bucket strategy, which involves dividing your retirement assets into different buckets with different investment goals and withdrawal timelines.

3. Tax planning: Withdrawals from some retirement accounts, such as traditional IRAs and 401(k)s, are subject to income tax. Consider working with a tax professional to develop a tax-efficient withdrawal strategy that minimizes your tax liability.

4. Required Minimum Distributions (RMDs): At age 72, you will be required to take minimum distributions from your traditional IRAs and 401(k)s. The amount of the distribution is based on your age

and the value of your retirement assets. Failure to take the required distribution can result in significant tax penalties, so be sure to understand and comply with RMD rules.

5. Estate planning: Finally, as you manage your retirement assets, it is important to consider how they will be distributed after your death. Work with an estate planning attorney to develop a plan that ensures your assets are distributed according to your wishes and that minimizes tax liabilities for your heirs.

8. Estate Planning and Wealth Transfer

Estate Planning and Wealth Transfer refer to the process of arranging for the transfer of an individual's assets after they pass away. It involves making important decisions about how assets are to be distributed, who will manage them, and how taxes and debts will be paid. Estate planning is important because it helps ensure that a person's wishes are followed after their death and that their assets are distributed in the most efficient and effective manner.

The process of estate planning involves several key steps. First, a person should create a comprehensive inventory of all their assets, including bank accounts, retirement accounts, real estate, and personal property. They should also compile a list of their liabilities, such as mortgages, credit card debt, and other outstanding loans.

The next step is to create a will or trust that outlines how the assets will be distributed after death. A will is a legal document that names beneficiaries and outlines the distribution of assets. A trust, on the other hand, is a legal entity that holds assets on behalf of beneficiaries. Trusts can offer several advantages over wills, including the ability to avoid probate and maintain greater control over how assets are distributed.

In addition to a will or trust, a person should also designate beneficiaries for their retirement accounts and life insurance policies. These assets pass outside of probate, so it is important to keep beneficiary designations up to date.

Estate planning also involves planning for potential incapacity. A person should consider creating a power of attorney or a healthcare directive to name someone to make financial and healthcare decisions on their behalf if they become unable to do so themselves.

Finally, estate planning involves considering the impact of taxes on the transfer of assets. A person may need to consider strategies such as gifting or setting up a trust to minimize tax liability.

Overall, estate planning and wealth transfer are important considerations for anyone with assets to their name. It is essential to consult with a qualified attorney or financial advisor to ensure that all the necessary steps are taken to protect and transfer assets according to a person's wishes.

Importance of estate planning for individuals and families

Estate planning is the process of preparing for the transfer of an individual's assets after their death. It involves making decisions about how one's assets will be distributed and managed in the event of incapacity or death. Estate planning is important for individuals and families for several reasons:

1. Protecting assets: Estate planning allows individuals to protect their assets and ensure that they are distributed according to their wishes.

2. Minimizing taxes: Proper estate planning can minimize taxes on an individual's assets, which can result in significant savings for their heirs.

3. Providing for loved ones: Estate planning allows individuals to provide for their loved ones after they are gone, by leaving assets to them directly or through a trust.

4. Ensuring continuity of business: For business owners, estate planning can ensure the continuity

of their business by providing for its transfer to a successor or heirs.

5. Avoiding probate: Proper estate planning can also help individuals avoid probate, which can be a lengthy and expensive process.

Overall, estate planning is important for individuals and families who want to ensure that their assets are managed and distributed according to their wishes, while also minimizing taxes and avoiding unnecessary legal complications.

Estate planning is the process of making a plan for the management and distribution of an individual's assets after their death. It involves deciding who will inherit what and making arrangements for any dependents, as well as specifying how any financial and legal matters should be handled.

There are several reasons why estate planning is important for individuals and families. First, it can help ensure that an individual's assets are distributed according to their wishes. Without an estate plan, the state will determine how assets are distributed, which may not align with an individual's wishes. Second, estate planning can help minimize taxes and legal fees that may arise during the distribution of assets. Third, estate planning can provide for the care of any dependents, such as children or elderly parents, after an individual's death. Finally, estate planning can help protect an individual's assets from potential creditors and lawsuits.

Overall, estate planning is a crucial component of financial planning for individuals and families. It can help provide peace of mind and ensure that an individual's assets are distributed in a way that aligns with their wishes.

Estate planning is crucial for individuals and families who want to ensure that their assets are transferred according to their wishes after their death. Without proper estate planning, one's assets may end up being distributed according to state laws, which may not align with their wishes. This can lead to disputes among family members and loved ones, as well as unnecessary expenses and taxes.

Estate planning involves several steps, including creating a will, setting up trusts, designating beneficiaries, and appointing guardians for minor children. These steps allow individuals to ensure that their assets are distributed according to their wishes, minimize estate taxes, and protect their assets from potential creditors.

Another important aspect of estate planning is wealth transfer. Wealth transfer refers to the process of transferring one's wealth to their beneficiaries in a tax-efficient manner. This can involve the use of trusts, gifting, and other strategies that allow individuals to transfer their assets to their beneficiaries while minimizing taxes.

Overall, estate planning and wealth transfer are important aspects of financial planning that individuals and families should consider to ensure that their wishes are carried out and their assets are protected. It's important to work with a qualified estate planning attorney or financial advisor to develop a comprehensive plan that meets your unique needs and goals.

Strategies for protecting assets and minimizing taxes

Estate planning involves creating a plan to manage your assets and distribute them after your death. One important aspect of estate planning is minimizing taxes on your assets to ensure that your heirs receive as much of your wealth as possible. Here are some strategies for protecting assets and minimizing taxes:

1. Establish a trust: A trust can help you protect assets from creditors and minimize taxes. You can set up a revocable trust during your lifetime, which allows you to retain control of the assets, or an irrevocable trust, which transfers ownership of the assets to the trust and removes them from your taxable estate.

2. Maximize use of annual gift tax exclusion: You can give up to $15,000 per person per year without incurring any gift tax. This can be a useful strategy for transferring assets to your heirs while you are still alive and reducing the size of your taxable estate.

3. Make charitable donations: Charitable donations can reduce your taxable estate while supporting causes you care about. You can make donations during your lifetime or include them in your estate plan.

4- Use life insurance: Life insurance can be used to provide liquidity for your estate and pay estate taxes. You can establish an irrevocable life insurance trust to hold the policy, which removes it from your taxable estate.

5. Consult with an estate planning attorney: An estate planning attorney can help you develop a comprehensive plan that meets your goals and minimizes taxes. They can also help you stay up to date with changes in tax laws and adjust your plan accordingly.

Estate planning involves creating a plan to manage and distribute a person's assets and properties after their death. This process can involve creating a will or trust, naming beneficiaries, and selecting individuals to manage the distribution of the assets. Estate planning can help protect assets and minimize taxes by utilizing various strategies such as trusts, gifting, and charitable donations.

One strategy for protecting assets is the creation of a trust, which is a legal arrangement in which a trustee manages assets for the benefit of the beneficiaries. Trusts can offer various benefits such as avoiding probate, protecting assets from creditors, and minimizing taxes.

Another strategy for minimizing taxes is through gifting, which involves giving away assets during a person's lifetime. Gift taxes are imposed on the value of the gift, but there are certain exemptions and exclusions that can help reduce the tax burden.

Charitable donations can also be a valuable estate planning strategy. Donating assets to a qualified charitable organization can provide tax benefits while also benefiting the charity.

Overall, estate planning and wealth transfer involve developing a comprehensive plan to protect assets and ensure their distribution according to a person's wishes. Seeking the advice of a financial planner or estate planning attorney can be beneficial in creating an effective plan that meets an individual's specific needs and goals.

Wealth transfer techniques and considerations

Wealth transfer refers to the process of transferring assets and wealth from one generation to another. It is an important aspect of estate planning, and there are various techniques and considerations to keep in mind when creating a wealth transfer plan.

One of the most common wealth transfer techniques is through gifting. Gifting allows individuals to transfer assets to their heirs during their lifetime, which can help to reduce the size of their estate and minimize estate taxes. There are annual gift tax exclusions that allow individuals to gift a certain amount to each recipient without incurring gift taxes, and there are also lifetime gift tax exemptions that can be used to transfer larger amounts.

Another technique is through the use of trusts. Trusts can be created to hold and manage assets for the benefit of future generations, and they can provide a number of benefits, including asset protection, tax savings, and flexibility in how assets are distributed. There are different types of trusts, such as revocable trusts, irrevocable trusts, and charitable trusts, each with its own advantages and disadvantages.

Considerations when creating a wealth transfer plan include the size and complexity of the estate, the goals and objectives of the individual, the needs of the heirs, and potential tax implications. It is important to work with a qualified estate planning attorney and financial advisor to ensure that the plan is legally sound, tax-efficient, and aligned with the individual's wishes.

Wealth transfer techniques and considerations involve various strategies to transfer assets from one generation to another. Here are some of the techniques used in wealth transfer:

1. Trusts: Trusts are legal documents that allow the grantor to transfer assets to a trustee to manage and distribute them to the beneficiaries according to the grantor's wishes. Trusts can be used to minimize estate taxes, avoid probate, and protect assets from creditors.

2. Gifting: Gifting is another technique that can be used to transfer wealth. An individual can gift up to $15,000 per year to each recipient without triggering gift taxes. Gifting can also be used as an

estate planning tool to reduce the size of an individual's taxable estate.

3. Family Limited Partnerships (FLPs): FLPs are a type of partnership that allows the transfer of assets to the next generation while retaining control of the assets. The partnership can be structured to minimize taxes and protect assets from creditors.

4. Life insurance: Life insurance is a common tool used in wealth transfer planning. It allows an individual to transfer assets to beneficiaries tax-free upon the individual's death.

When considering wealth transfer, it is important to take into account various considerations, such as the size of the estate, the type of assets, the number of beneficiaries, and the tax implications. Working with a financial advisor or estate planning attorney can help individuals determine the most appropriate wealth transfer techniques for their specific situation.

Preparing for end-of-life decisions

Preparing for end-of-life decisions is an important aspect of estate planning. This involves making sure that your wishes are carried out in the event of your death or incapacity. Some of the key considerations in end-of-life planning include:

1. Advance directives: Advance directives are legal documents that specify your wishes regarding medical treatment and end-of-life care. These include living wills and healthcare proxies, which designate someone to make healthcare decisions on your behalf if you are unable to do so.

2. Estate planning documents: Estate planning documents, such as wills and trusts, are important for ensuring that your assets are distributed according to your wishes. They can also help minimize the taxes and fees associated with transferring assets to your heirs.

3. Beneficiary designations: Many types of assets, such as retirement accounts and life insurance policies, allow you to designate a beneficiary to receive the assets upon your death. It's important

to review these designations regularly and make sure they reflect your current wishes.

4. Organ donation: If you wish to donate your organs, it's important to discuss this with your family and include your wishes in your advance directives.

5. Funeral and burial arrangements: You may also wish to plan for your funeral and burial arrangements, including whether you would like to be cremated or buried, and any specific instructions or preferences you may have.

Overall, end-of-life planning is an important aspect of estate planning that can help ensure that your wishes are carried out and your loved ones are provided for. It's important to work with a qualified estate planning attorney and financial advisor to develop a comprehensive plan that reflects your wishes and meets your needs.

End-of-life decisions can be difficult and emotional to make, but it is important to plan ahead for them to ensure that your wishes are carried out and that your loved ones are not left with undue burdens.

Estate planning plays a critical role in preparing for end-of-life decisions.

One of the most important aspects of end-of-life planning is creating a will or trust. This legal document outlines how your assets should be distributed after you pass away. A will can also appoint guardians for any minor children and specify any last wishes, such as funeral arrangements. Without a will or trust, your assets will be distributed according to the laws of your state, which may not align with your wishes.

Another important aspect of end-of-life planning is creating advance directives. These legal documents outline your wishes for medical treatment if you become incapacitated and unable to make decisions for yourself. They typically include a living will, which specifies the types of life-sustaining treatments you do or do not want, and a healthcare power of attorney, which designates someone to make medical decisions on your behalf.

It is also important to consider long-term care planning as part of your end-of-life preparations. This includes planning for any potential long-term care needs and considering options for paying for that care, such as long-term care insurance.

Finally, you should consider consulting with an estate planning attorney to ensure that your wishes are legally documented and your assets are protected. They can also help you navigate complex tax laws and other legal considerations that may impact your end-of-life plans.

9. Conclusion (1): Putting It All Together

Putting all of these personal finance topics together is the key to achieving financial success and security. It's important to have a comprehensive understanding of each area and how they relate to one another in order to create a solid financial plan.

Start by assessing your current financial situation and identifying areas where you can make improvements. This may involve setting goals for debt reduction, increasing your savings, or developing a retirement plan.

Next, create a budget that takes into account all of your income and expenses, including debt payments and savings contributions. Stick to your budget as closely as possible and adjust it as needed to accommodate any changes in your income or expenses.

As you work on your budget, focus on building an emergency fund to cover unexpected expenses and consider investing in a diversified portfolio of assets to help grow your wealth over time.

If you're a business owner or entrepreneur, be sure to prioritize proper planning, financing, and growth strategies to ensure the long-term success of your company.

Finally, don't forget about important topics such as estate planning and wealth transfer, as well as end-of-life decisions. These can be difficult topics to discuss, but they are critical for ensuring your wishes are followed and your loved ones are taken care of after you're gone.

By taking a holistic approach to personal finance and considering all of these important topics, you can create a solid foundation for financial success and security both now and in the future.

Throughout this comprehensive guide, we have covered a wide range of personal finance topics, from budgeting and saving to investing and estate planning. While each area is important in its own right, it is essential to understand how they all fit together and can be integrated into an overall financial plan.

To recap some of the key strategies and techniques covered in this guide:

- Budgeting: creating and sticking to a budget is the foundation of personal finance. It allows you to track your income and expenses and make informed financial decisions.

- Saving: building an emergency fund, contributing to retirement accounts, and investing in a diversified portfolio are all key ways to grow your wealth over time.

- Credit and debt management: understanding your credit score and reports, responsible use of credit cards, and paying off debt faster are all strategies for improving your financial health and avoiding costly mistakes.

- Real estate and homeownership: weighing the pros and cons of buying vs. renting, taking steps to qualify for a mortgage, and managing your mortgage effectively are all important aspects of building long-term wealth through real estate.

- Starting and growing a business: assessing your business idea and market viability, financing your business, managing cash flow and finances, and scaling your business over time are all critical components of building a successful business.

- Planning for retirement: understanding different retirement plans, maximizing retirement savings, and managing retirement assets and withdrawals are all essential for preparing for a comfortable and secure retirement.

- Estate planning and wealth transfer: protecting assets, minimizing taxes, and preparing for end-of-life decisions are important considerations for ensuring that your wealth is distributed according to your wishes.

By implementing these strategies and techniques, you can take control of your finances and build a solid foundation for your future. Remember that financial planning is a journey, not a destination, and that there will be bumps in the road along the way. But with a solid plan in place and a commitment to making smart financial decisions, you can achieve your goals and live the life you want.

Congratulations on making it this far and learning about various aspects of personal finance! The knowledge you have gained is a powerful tool that can help you take control of your financial future.

To recap, some of the key strategies and techniques we covered include:

1. Creating a budget and tracking your expenses to gain a better understanding of your financial situation.

2. Saving for emergencies and unexpected expenses to avoid going into debt.

3. Building a diversified investment portfolio to maximize returns and minimize risk.

4. Understanding credit scores and reports to improve your creditworthiness and responsible use of credit cards to avoid high-interest debt.

5. Considering the advantages and disadvantages of buying vs. renting when it comes to real estate.

6. Assessing the viability of your business idea, identifying financing options, managing cash flow and finances, and developing a strategy for scaling and growing your business.

7. Understanding the different retirement plans available, maximizing retirement savings, and preparing for retirement income and expenses.

8. Creating an estate plan to protect your assets and minimize taxes, transfer your wealth, and prepare for end-of-life decisions.

It can be overwhelming to implement all of these strategies at once, but the key is to start small and make progress over time. Set achievable goals and create a plan to achieve them. Don't hesitate to seek the help of financial professionals or use online resources to guide you along the way.

Remember that improving your financial life is a journey, not a destination. By taking small steps and making incremental changes, you can achieve long-term financial success and security.

In conclusion, financial literacy is essential for building wealth, achieving financial stability, and securing a comfortable retirement. Whether you are just starting out in your career or nearing retirement age, there are always steps you can take to improve your financial situation.

Throughout this guide, we have covered a wide range of financial topics, including budgeting, saving, investing, credit and debt management, real estate, retirement planning, and estate planning. By understanding these concepts and implementing the strategies and techniques discussed, you can take control of your finances and achieve your financial goals.

Remember that financial success is not a one-time event, but a lifelong journey. It requires ongoing learning, discipline, and commitment. As you continue to develop your financial literacy, it's important to stay informed about changes in the economy, tax laws, and financial markets.

There are many resources available to help you on your financial journey, including financial advisors, online courses, books, podcasts, and blogs. Take advantage of these resources and continue to invest in your financial education.

Finally, remember that financial success is not just about accumulating wealth but also about achieving a sense of financial security, freedom, and peace of mind. By taking control of your finances and making smart decisions, you can build a more prosperous and fulfilling life for yourself and your loved ones.

10. Bonus Chapter: Tips for Building Wealth

Mindset shifts for building wealth

Here are some mindset shifts that can help you build wealth:

1. Embrace a long-term perspective: Building wealth takes time, so it's important to think in terms of years or even decades rather than months or weeks.

2. Focus on opportunities, not obstacles: Instead of dwelling on the challenges that you face, try to identify the opportunities that exist in any given situation.

3. Embrace learning and growth: The more you learn and grow, the more opportunities you will have to build wealth.

4. Develop a positive relationship with money: This means viewing money as a tool that can help you achieve your goals, rather than an end in itself.

5. Take calculated risks: Building wealth often requires taking calculated risks, such as investing in stocks or starting a business.

6. Surround yourself with like-minded people: Surrounding yourself with people who share your goals and values can help keep you motivated and accountable.

7. Be patient and persistent: Building wealth is a marathon, not a sprint. It requires patience, persistence, and a willingness to keep moving forward even when things get tough.

By adopting these mindset shifts, you can begin to approach wealth-building with a more positive and productive attitude, which can help you achieve your financial goals over time.

Strategies for increasing income

Here are some strategies that can help increase your income:

1. Negotiate your salary: If you feel that you are not being paid enough, you can always try to negotiate with your employer for a better salary. Make sure to do your research and present a compelling case for why you deserve a raise.

2. Start a side hustle: You can also consider starting a side business or offering freelance services to supplement your income. This can be done on a part-time basis, and you can gradually grow your business over time.

3. Invest in your education: Consider investing in your education by taking courses or certifications that can help you acquire new skills and increase your market value. This can help you get better-paying jobs or start a business in a field that you are passionate about.

4. Look for passive income opportunities: Consider investing in stocks, real estate, or other passive income opportunities that can generate income for you while you focus on other things.

5. Find a better job: If you feel that your current job is not offering you the opportunities you need to grow your income, you can always look for a better job that offers better pay and benefits.

Remember, building wealth is not an overnight process, and it requires discipline, hard work, and patience. By adopting these strategies and being consistent with your efforts, you can gradually increase your income and build a solid financial foundation for yourself and your family.

Techniques for saving money on everyday expenses

Here are some techniques for saving money on everyday expenses:

1. Budgeting: Creating a budget is an essential part of managing your money effectively. Knowing where your money is going each month helps you identify areas where you can cut back and save.

2. Couponing: Using coupons can save you a lot of money on groceries, household items, and other essentials. Look for coupons in your local newspaper, online, or in-store.

3. Meal planning: Planning your meals ahead of time can help you save money on groceries by avoiding impulse purchases and reducing food waste. It also makes it easier to cook at home and avoid expensive takeout meals.

4. Buying in bulk: Buying in bulk can be a great way to save money on items that you use frequently,

such as toilet paper, cleaning supplies, and non-perishable food items.

5. Shopping around: Don't assume that the first price you see is the best price. Shop around for the best deals, and compare prices at different stores to get the best value for your money.

6. Negotiating: Don't be afraid to negotiate when making big purchases, such as a car or home. You may be able to get a better price or a better deal by negotiating with the seller.

7. Using cashback and rewards programs: Using cashback and rewards programs can help you earn money back on purchases that you would make anyway. Look for credit cards or loyalty programs that offer cashback, points, or other rewards for your spending.

By implementing these techniques and making a conscious effort to save money on everyday expenses, you can free up more money to put towards your financial goals and build wealth over time.

Building passive income streams

Building passive income streams is a great way to supplement your regular income and build long-term wealth. Passive income is money that you earn without having to actively work for it. Here are some techniques for building passive income streams:

1. Rental Properties: Owning and renting out properties can provide a steady stream of passive income. You can rent out a room in your home, or purchase a property solely for the purpose of renting it out. This can be a great way to build wealth over time.

2. Dividend-Paying Stocks: Dividend-paying stocks are a great way to generate passive income. These stocks pay out regular dividends to shareholders, which can provide a steady source of income.

3. Peer-to-Peer Lending: Peer-to-peer lending platforms like LendingClub and Prosper allow you to lend money to individuals and businesses in exchange for interest payments. This can be a great

way to generate passive income while helping others.

4. Creating and Selling Digital Products: If you have a skill or expertise in a particular area, you can create digital products like eBooks, courses, or tutorials, and sell them online. Once you've created the product, you can continue to earn income from it without having to do any additional work.

5. Affiliate Marketing: Affiliate marketing involves promoting other people's products and earning a commission on any sales that result from your promotion. This can be done through a blog, social media, or other online platforms.

It's important to remember that building passive income streams takes time and effort. It's not a quick fix for financial stability or wealth. However, if you're willing to put in the work and be patient, passive income streams can be a great way to build long-term wealth and financial security.

11. Bonus Chapter: Navigating Financial Challenges

Navigating Financial Challenges refers to the process of managing unexpected financial setbacks or obstacles that may occur in one's life. These challenges can be caused by a variety of factors, such as job loss, medical expenses, unexpected home or car repairs, and other emergencies. While it can be challenging to navigate these difficulties, there are several strategies and techniques that can help individuals and families overcome financial challenges and emerge stronger and more resilient.

Here are some tips for navigating financial challenges:

1. Create a Budget: A budget can help you track your income and expenses, and identify areas where you can reduce spending. It can also help you prioritize your expenses and allocate resources towards important items, such as savings or debt payments.

2. Build an Emergency Fund: Having an emergency fund can help you prepare for unexpected

expenses and provide a cushion during difficult times. Aim to save at least 3-6 months of living expenses in an easily accessible savings account.

3. Negotiate Payment Plans: If you're struggling to pay bills or debts, reach out to creditors and ask about payment plans or hardship programs. Many lenders are willing to work with you to develop a plan that suits your needs.

4. Consider Debt Consolidation: If you have multiple high-interest debts, consolidating them into a single loan or credit line with a lower interest rate can help you save money and simplify your payments.

5. Seek Professional Help: If you're struggling to manage your finances or debt on your own, consider seeking professional help. Financial planners, credit counselors, and debt management services can provide guidance and support to help you navigate your financial challenges.

6. Prioritize Self-Care: Financial challenges can be stressful and emotionally draining. Prioritizing self-care activities, such as exercise, meditation, or

spending time with loved ones, can help you manage stress and maintain a positive outlook.

Remember, navigating financial challenges requires patience, persistence, and a willingness to learn and adapt. By taking proactive steps and seeking help when needed, you can overcome obstacles and build a stronger financial foundation for the future.

Navigating financial challenges can be difficult, but it's essential to be prepared and have a plan to handle them. Financial challenges can come in many forms, such as job loss, unexpected expenses, medical emergencies, market downturns, and more. These challenges can create stress and uncertainty, but with the right mindset and approach, you can overcome them.

One of the first steps to navigating financial challenges is to assess your current financial situation. Take a look at your income, expenses, debts, savings, and investments. This will help you understand your financial strengths and weaknesses and identify areas that need improvement. It's also essential to have an emergency fund to cover unexpected expenses or financial setbacks.

Another critical aspect of navigating financial challenges is to prioritize your expenses. Start by covering your essential needs, such as housing, food, and healthcare. Then, focus on paying off high-interest debts and building up your savings. If you have a budget, review it to see if there are any areas where you can cut back on expenses to save money.

When dealing with financial challenges, it's essential to seek help and support when needed. Don't be afraid to reach out to a financial advisor, credit counselor, or other financial professional for guidance and advice. They can help you create a plan to address your financial challenges and navigate them successfully.

Finally, it's important to stay positive and maintain a growth mindset. Financial challenges can be daunting, but they also present opportunities for learning and growth. With perseverance and a positive attitude, you can overcome financial challenges and achieve your financial goals.

Financial setbacks and unexpected expenses can happen to anyone, regardless of how well they plan and manage their finances. These situations can be stressful and overwhelming, but there are strategies you can use to help you navigate through them.

First, it's important to have an emergency fund. This fund should ideally have three to six months' worth of living expenses set aside to cover unexpected expenses or a sudden loss of income. If you don't have an emergency fund, start building one as soon as possible.

If you're dealing with debt during difficult times, prioritize paying off high-interest debt first. Consider consolidating your debt or speaking with a credit counselor to come up with a plan to pay off your debt.

During job loss or an economic downturn, it's important to remain proactive and take steps to maintain your financial stability. Consider looking for additional sources of income, such as part-time work or freelance opportunities. You may also need to cut back on expenses and prioritize your bills.

It's also important to communicate with your creditors or lenders if you're struggling to make payments. They may be able to work out a payment plan or offer temporary relief options.

Remember to take care of your mental health during these difficult times as well. Seek support from loved ones or a mental health professional if needed.

Overall, the key to navigating financial challenges is to stay proactive, communicate with your creditors or lenders, prioritize your expenses, and take care of your mental health.

12. Bonus Chapter: Investing in Yourself

Investing in yourself is the act of spending time, energy, and resources on your personal and professional growth. This involves enhancing your knowledge, skills, and abilities through various means such as education, training, coaching, mentorship, and self-reflection. Investing in yourself is essential because it allows you to expand your potential and achieve greater success in all areas of your life.

Personal and professional development is important because it helps you to:

1. Increase your self-awareness: By investing in yourself, you can learn more about your strengths, weaknesses, and personal values. This self-awareness can help you make better decisions and communicate more effectively with others.

2. Develop new skills: Whether it's learning a new language, improving your writing skills, or developing your leadership abilities, investing in yourself allows you to acquire new skills that can

enhance your career prospects and personal growth.

3. Build your confidence: Investing in yourself can help you build your self-esteem and confidence. As you develop new skills and acquire new knowledge, you become more confident in your abilities, which can help you take on new challenges and achieve your goals.

4. Improve your relationships: Personal and professional development can also help you improve your relationships with others. As you become more self-aware and develop new skills, you can communicate more effectively and build stronger, more meaningful relationships with others.

5. Increase your earning potential: By investing in yourself and acquiring new skills and knowledge, you can increase your earning potential and career opportunities.

There are many ways to invest in yourself, including:

1. Reading books and taking courses: Reading books and taking courses can help you acquire new knowledge and skills, as well as expose you to new perspectives and ideas.

2. Attending conferences and events: Attending conferences and events can help you network with others in your field and learn about the latest trends and innovations.

3. Hiring a coach or mentor: A coach or mentor can provide you with guidance, feedback, and support as you work towards your goals.

4. Joining professional associations or clubs: Joining professional associations or clubs can help you network with others in your field and stay up-to-date on the latest news and developments.

5. Traveling: Traveling can expose you to new cultures and perspectives, as well as help you develop problem-solving and adaptability skills.

Overall, investing in yourself is a crucial aspect of personal and professional growth. By taking the time to learn, develop new skills, and explore new opportunities, you can expand your potential and achieve greater success in all areas of your life.

Investing in education and skill-building is crucial for personal and professional growth. Here are some strategies for investing in yourself through education and skill-building:

1. Attend workshops and conferences: Attending workshops and conferences can help you stay up to date on the latest trends and best practices in your industry. It's also a great way to network with other professionals and learn from their experiences.

2. Take online courses: There are many online courses available in a variety of subjects. Online learning platforms such as Coursera, Udemy, and LinkedIn Learning offer courses in everything from data analysis to digital marketing.

3. Pursue advanced degrees: If you're looking to advance your career, pursuing an advanced degree

can be a great way to gain new skills and knowledge. Graduate programs in business, engineering, healthcare, and other fields can help you take your career to the next level.

4. Learn new skills: Learning new skills can be a great way to expand your knowledge and increase your value as an employee. Whether it's coding, public speaking, or a foreign language, learning new skills can help you stand out in a crowded job market.

5. Read books: Reading books is a great way to learn new ideas and gain insights from experts in your field. It's also a great way to improve your critical thinking skills and expand your worldview.

Investing in yourself through education and skill-building can pay off in many ways, including career advancement, higher earning potential, and personal fulfillment.

Building a personal brand and monetizing your expertise is becoming increasingly important in today's digital age, where social media and online platforms have made it easier than ever to showcase your skills and knowledge to a wide audience.

To start building your personal brand, you need to identify your unique skills and expertise, as well as your target audience. You can do this by conducting a self-audit to determine what you're good at and what sets you apart from others in your field. Once you have a clear understanding of your skills and expertise, you can start to build your online presence by creating a website, social media profiles, and other digital assets that showcase your skills and expertise.

To monetize your expertise, you can offer services such as coaching, consulting, or training to individuals or businesses in your industry. You can also create digital products such as e-books, courses, or webinars that offer value to your target audience. Additionally, you can explore affiliate marketing or sponsored content opportunities, where you promote products or services to your audience and earn a commission on sales or clicks.

Investing in yourself by building a personal brand and monetizing your expertise can provide numerous benefits, including increased visibility, credibility, and income potential. By establishing yourself as an expert in your field, you can also open up new opportunities for career advancement and personal growth.

Creating multiple streams of income is an effective way to diversify your income sources and increase your earning potential. Here are some tips for creating multiple streams of income:

1. Identify your skills and passions: Consider your hobbies, interests, and skills and see if there are opportunities to monetize them. For example, if you enjoy writing, you could start freelance writing for online publications or start your own blog.

2. Start a side business: Starting a side business can be a great way to create an additional stream of income. Consider your expertise and see if there is a market for a product or service related to it.

3. Invest in real estate: Investing in real estate can provide a reliable stream of passive income. Consider purchasing rental properties or investing in real estate investment trusts (REITs).

4. Participate in the gig economy: With the rise of the gig economy, there are many opportunities to earn money through freelance work or short-term contracts. Consider driving for a ride-sharing

service or delivering food for a food delivery service.

5. Invest in stocks and other investments: Investing in stocks, mutual funds, and other investments can provide a steady stream of passive income over time. However, it's important to do your research and make informed investment decisions.

6. Create digital products: With the rise of e-commerce and digital products, there are many opportunities to create and sell digital products such as e-books, courses, and software.

7. Rent out assets: Consider renting out assets such as your car, parking space, or even your home on a short-term rental platform like Airbnb.

Remember that creating multiple streams of income requires effort and dedication. It's important to focus on building income streams that align with your skills and interests, and to continually evaluate and adjust your strategy as needed.

13. Conclusion:

Taking Action for Lasting Change

Taking action for lasting change is critical for achieving financial success and building wealth. It is not enough to have knowledge and information; it must be put into action. Here are some tips to help you take action and make lasting changes in your financial life:

1. Set clear goals: Identify specific and measurable financial goals that you want to achieve. Write them down and make a plan to achieve them.

2. Create a budget: A budget is an essential tool for managing your money and achieving your financial goals. It helps you track your spending and ensure that you are living within your means.

3. Pay off debt: Debt can be a significant barrier to building wealth. Create a plan to pay off your debt, starting with high-interest debt first.

4. Save and invest: Saving and investing your money is essential for building wealth over time. Make it a habit to save a portion of your income each month and invest in a diversified portfolio.

5. Take calculated risks: Building wealth often involves taking risks. However, it is important to take calculated risks, not reckless ones. Do your research and seek advice from experts before making any investment decisions.

6. Learn from failures: Failure is an inevitable part of the journey to success. Instead of giving up, use failures as an opportunity to learn and grow. Identify what went wrong and make adjustments to your plan.

7. Stay motivated: Building wealth takes time and requires patience and discipline. Stay motivated by celebrating your successes along the way and reminding yourself of your long-term goals.

Remember that taking action for lasting change is a continuous process. Keep learning, adjusting, and making progress towards your goals, and you will be on your way to financial success and building lasting wealth.

In summary, the book covers various aspects of personal finance and wealth building, including budgeting, debt management, saving, investing, retirement planning, estate planning, and personal development. The key takeaways include:

1. Developing a growth mindset and taking ownership of your financial situation is crucial for achieving financial success.

2. Creating a budget and sticking to it is an essential first step in taking control of your finances.

3. Reducing debt, building an emergency fund, and saving for retirement are important for long-term financial stability.

4. Investing in assets that appreciate over time and generating passive income can help you build wealth.

5. Planning for retirement and estate transfer is necessary to ensure that your financial legacy is preserved.

6. Overcoming financial challenges such as unexpected expenses, job loss, and economic downturns requires a resilient mindset and a plan of action.

7. Personal and professional development can help you increase your earning potential and create additional streams of income.

8. Taking consistent action towards your financial goals, using the strategies outlined in the book, can lead to lasting change and financial freedom.

By implementing the strategies outlined in this book, you can take control of your finances, build wealth, and achieve your financial goals. Remember that the key to success is taking consistent action and staying committed to your financial plan.

To implement changes in your financial life, here are some practical steps to take:

1. Set specific goals: Identify what you want to achieve financially, such as saving for a down payment on a house, paying off debt, or building an emergency fund. Make sure your goals are specific, measurable, achievable, relevant, and time-bound (SMART).

2. Create a budget: Develop a budget that reflects your income and expenses, and identify areas where you can cut back on spending.

3. Reduce debt: Develop a debt reduction plan by prioritizing high-interest debt and making extra payments to reduce balances.

4. Invest for the future: Start investing for the future by contributing to a retirement account or other investment vehicles.

5. Continuously learn and improve: Keep learning about personal finance and financial planning

through books, podcasts, courses, and other resources.

6. Seek professional advice: Consider working with a financial advisor or planner who can provide personalized advice and guidance.

7. Take action: Start taking steps towards your financial goals today. Create a plan, stick to it, and make adjustments as needed to ensure you stay on track.

Remember that making changes in your financial life requires discipline, dedication, and commitment. It may take time to see results, but by taking action and implementing these steps, you can achieve lasting change and improve your financial future.

It's one thing to read about financial strategies and techniques, but it's another thing entirely to take action and implement them in your own life. The most important thing you can do is to start taking small steps towards your financial goals today.

One of the best ways to stay motivated is to remind yourself of the benefits that achieving your financial goals will bring. Maybe you want to save for a down payment on a house, pay off debt, or retire comfortably. Whatever your goals may be, keep them in mind as you take action.

It's also important to find an accountability partner or a community of like-minded individuals who can support you on your journey. This can be a financial advisor, a mentor, a friend, or an online group.

Remember, financial success is a journey, not a destination. It takes time, effort, and discipline to achieve your goals, but with the right mindset and strategies in place, you can take control of your financial future and create lasting change.

"It is important to rate books that we read, as it not only provides valuable feedback to the author but also helps other readers make informed decisions about whether to read the book or not. Rating a book can also contribute to its success and impact in the literary world. Your honest rating and review can make a significant difference in the author's career and encourage them to keep writing. So, if you enjoyed this book, don't forget to rate it and share your thoughts with others. Your feedback can make a big difference!"

Made in the USA
Las Vegas, NV
11 November 2024